You Can Draw

Trucks

By Mark Bergin

Contents

You Can Draw

Trucks

SALARIYA

Published in Great Britain in MMXII by
Book House, an imprint of
The Salariya Book Company Ltd
25 Marlborough Place, Brighton BN1 1UB

1 3 5 7 9 8 6 4 2

Please visit our websites at **www.salariya.com** or
www.book-house.co.uk for **free** electronic versions of:
You Wouldn't Want to Be an Egyptian Mummy!
You Wouldn't Want to Be a Roman Gladiator!
You Wouldn't Want to be a Polar Explorer!
You Wouldn't Want to Sail on a 19th-Century
Whaling Ship!

Author: Mark Bergin was born in Hastings in 1961. He
studied at Eastbourne College of Art and has specialised
in historical reconstructions as well as aviation and
maritime subjects since 1983. He lives in Bexhill-on-
Sea with his wife and three children.

Editor: Rob Walker

PB ISBN: 978-1-908759-54-2

A CIP catalogue record for this book is available from
the British Library.

Printed and bound in China.
Printed on paper from sustainable sources.

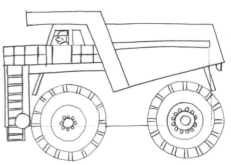

PAPER FROM
SUSTAINABLE
FORESTS

Visit our **new** online shop at

shop.salariya.com

for great offers, gift ideas, all our new releases

and free postage and packaging.

Introduction

Learning to draw is fun. In this book a finished drawing will be broken up into stages as a guide to completing your own drawing. However, this is only the beginning. The more you practise, the better you will get. Have fun coming up with cool designs, adding more incredible details and using new materials to achieve different effects!

This is an example showing how each drawing will be built up in easy stages. New sections of the drawing will be shown in colour to make each additional step clear.

1

2

3

4

5

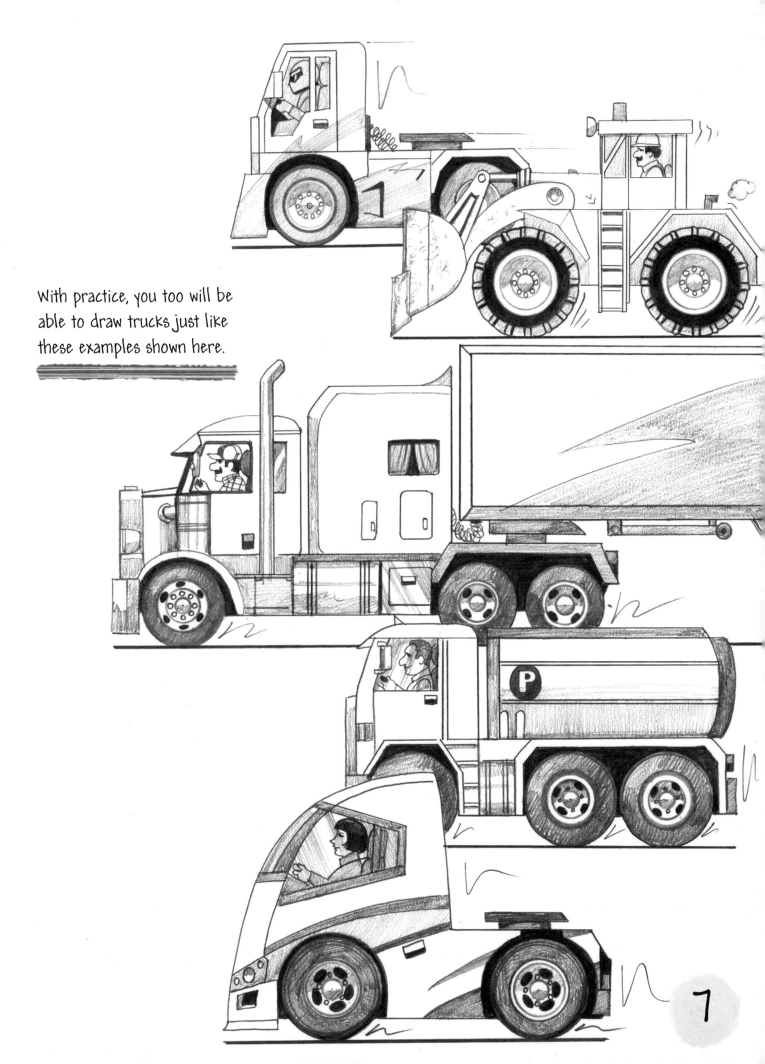

With practice, you too will be
able to draw trucks just like
these examples shown here.

Materials

There are many different art materials available which you can use to draw and colour in your vehicles. Try out each one for new and exciting results. The more you practise with them, the better your drawing skills will get!

Use a pencil to draw the shape of your truck. Any mistakes you make can easily be erased, as can any construction lines that are left over at the end of your drawing.

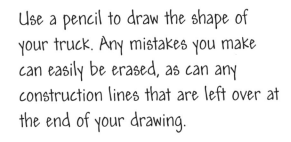

An eraser can be used to rub out any pencil mistakes. It can also be used to create highlights on pencil drawings.

You can go over your finished pencil lines with pen to make the lines bolder. But remember, a pen line is permanent so you can't erase any mistakes!

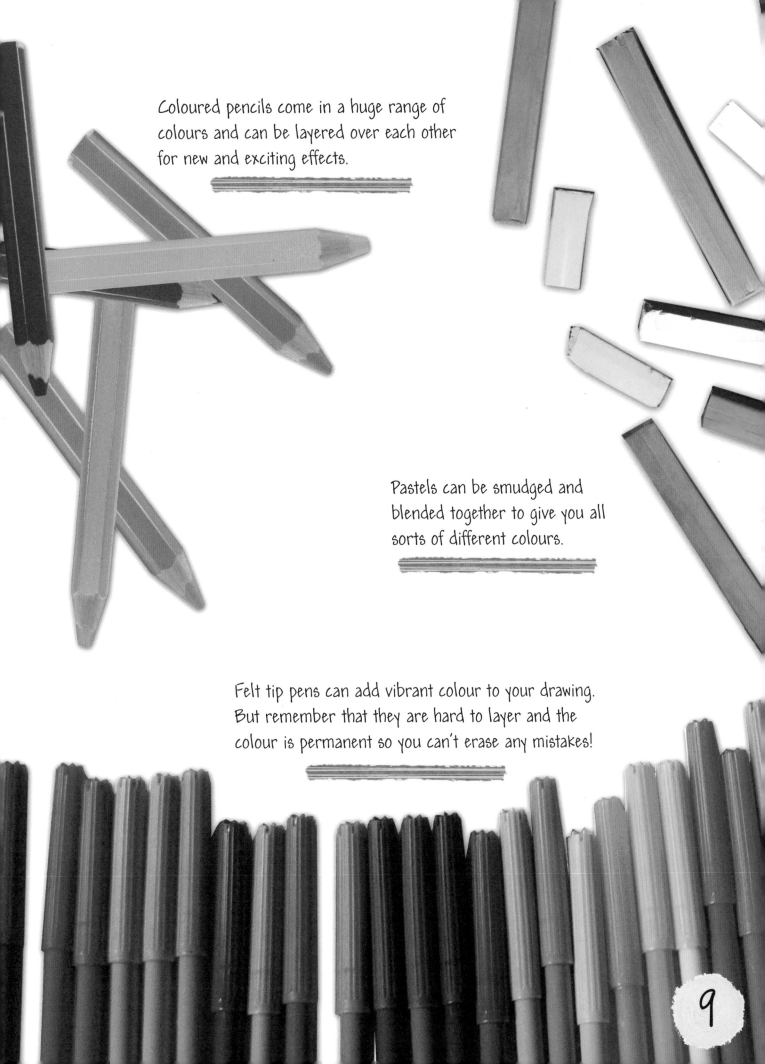

Coloured pencils come in a huge range of colours and can be layered over each other for new and exciting effects.

Pastels can be smudged and blended together to give you all sorts of different colours.

Felt tip pens can add vibrant colour to your drawing. But remember that they are hard to layer and the colour is permanent so you can't erase any mistakes!

Inspiration

Many types of trucks are made throughout the world. You can choose any of them as the inspiration for your cartoon-style drawing. Photos, magazines or books can give you new ideas and new designs to try.

When turning your truck into a cartoon-style, two-dimensional drawing, concentrate on the key elements you want to include and the overall shape of the truck.

One way to make your truck look cool is to exaggerate its key features and perhaps add new ones!

Use different colours and designs to make your truck look the way you want it to. It's your creation after all.

Concrete mixer

A concrete mixer is a specially adapted truck used to transport concrete. The rear container rotates constantly to stop the concrete from setting hard.

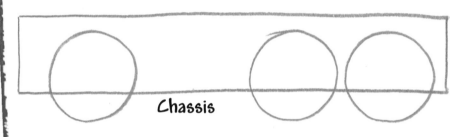

Chassis

Draw three circles for the wheels. Add an overlapping rectangle for the chassis.

Draw in the basic shape of the driver's cab.

Rotating mixer

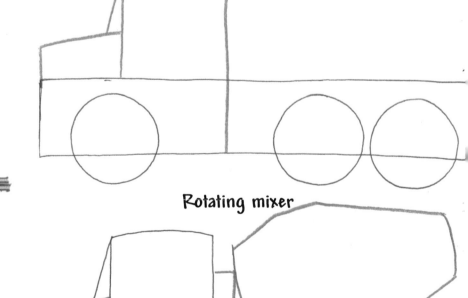

Add inner circles to the wheels for hubcaps. Draw in the large, rotating mixer.

Draw in the cab window and door. Add the front grill. Draw in the wheel arches and add lines to the rotating mixer.

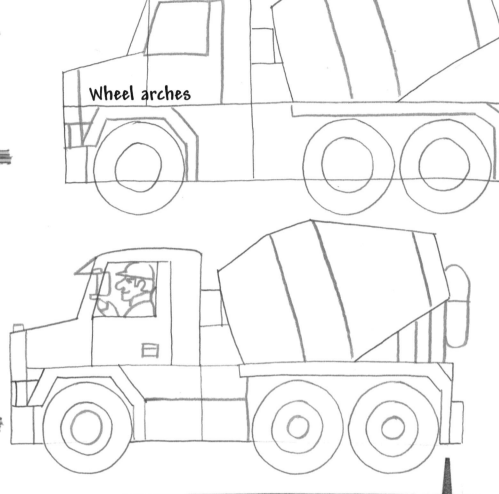

Wheel arches

Add the driver, wing mirror and door handle. Extend the cab roof at the front and add another circle to each hubcap. Draw in the details at the back of the rotating mixer.

Now add colour to the bodywork of your concrete mixer. Complete any final details.

Truck

This truck has a special coupling mechanism that attaches to large trailers so it can haul them over long distances.

Draw three circles for the wheels, with an overlapping rectangle for the chassis.

Add the driver's cab to the front half of the chassis.

Draw in three more circles for the inner wheel. Add the windows.

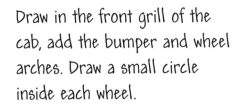
Draw in the front grill of the cab, add the bumper and wheel arches. Draw a small circle inside each wheel.

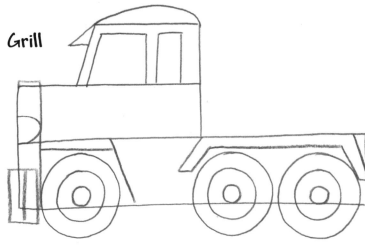

Exhaust

Coupling

Draw in the driver, wing mirror, exhaust pipe and hubcap. Add the trailer coupling.

Finish your drawing by completing all the remaining details and adding colour.

Snow plough

A snow plough has a large blade attached to the front which is used to move huge piles of snow.

Draw three circles for wheels and add a long rectangle for the chassis.

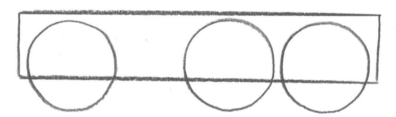

Draw in a large box shape on top of the chassis for the body. Add dividing lines.

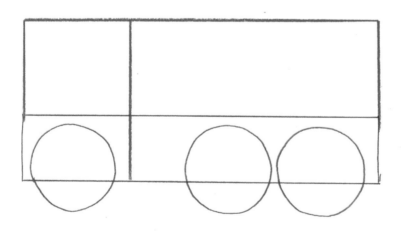

Draw in the window and divide the rear trailer into sections.

Draw in window details and add sections to the trailer. Add two more circles to the wheels for the hubcaps.

Draw the snow plough blade at the front of the vehicle. Add the driver, the exhaust, the wheel arches and other small details.

To complete your drawing add snow to the tyres and some heaped in front of the blade. Finish all extra details, then add colour to your drawing.

17

Racing truck

Racing trucks are normal haulage trucks that have been stripped down and their engines tuned up for speed. It's very exciting when these big machines race together.

Draw two circles for the wheels. Add an overlapping rectangle for the chassis.

Add the shape of the driver's cab and the shape of the door.

Add the front bumper, wheel arch and extra circles for the hubcaps.

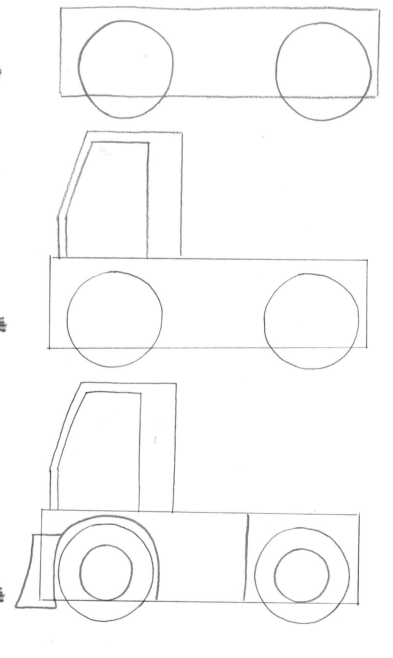

Draw in the front grill, window sections and rear wheel arch. Add two small circles to the wheels.

Draw in the driver and add details to the cab: wing mirror, exhaust and door handle. Draw in the different hubcaps, the trailer coupling, the rear lights and other small details.

Add colour to your racing truck – try making up a racing design of your own! Add any extra details you wish.

Monster truck

This crazy truck has huge wheels so it can climb over large objects, even cars!

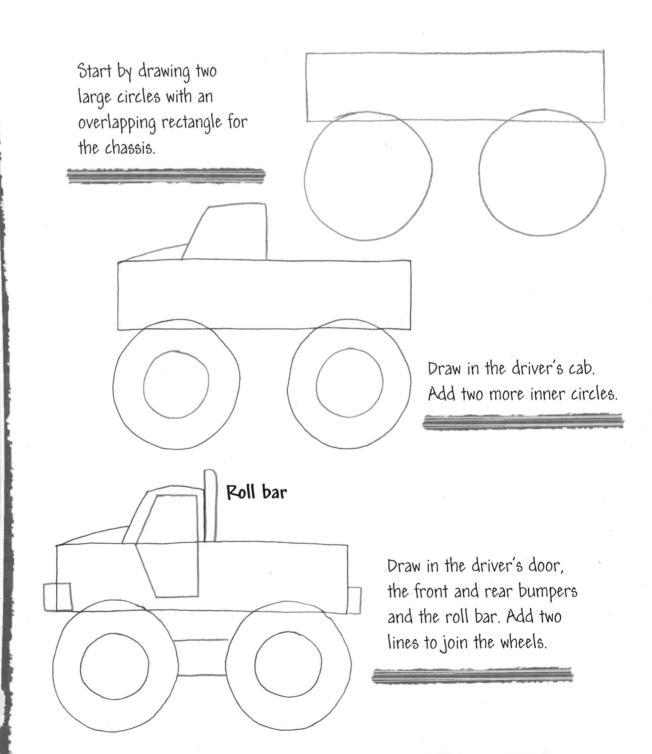

Start by drawing two large circles with an overlapping rectangle for the chassis.

Draw in the driver's cab. Add two more inner circles.

Roll bar

Draw in the driver's door, the front and rear bumpers and the roll bar. Add two lines to join the wheels.

Shock absorber

Add the front grill and the wheel arches (including the giant shock absorbers). Complete the roll bar.

Draw in the driver and add cab details. Add diagonal lines to the shock absorbers. Draw another circle onto each hubcap and add the wheel nuts.

Complete all remaining details, then add mud to the wheels and a cool design on the bodywork. Finish your drawing by colouring it in.

21

Pickup truck

This classic old truck is used to move small loads or even small livestock like sheep!

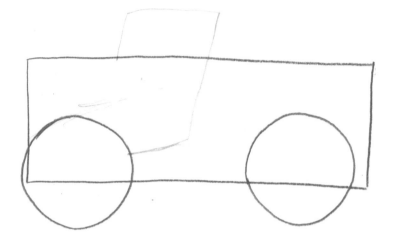

Draw two circles for the wheels and add an overlapping rectangle for the chassis.

Add a small rectangle for the driver's cab.

Pickup section

Add the roof and the pickup section at the rear. Draw in the front and rear bumpers.

Add in the front grill and draw in the differently-shaped wheel arches. Add a window to the cab and circles for hubcaps.

Add the driver, the front headlight and engine details. Complete the wooden framework at the rear and add the wheel nuts.

Finish off your truck by colouring in your drawing and adding any small design details.

Digger

A large bucket with pneumatic arms is attached to the front of a digger. This can scoop out soil from the ground and move it elsewhere.

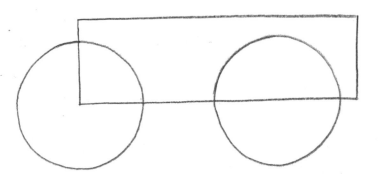

Draw in two circles for the wheels and add a long rectangle which starts halfway through the first circle and overlaps the second.

Add an extension to the rectangle. Draw in the rear shape of the digger.

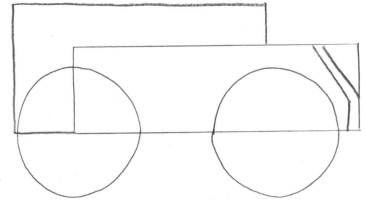

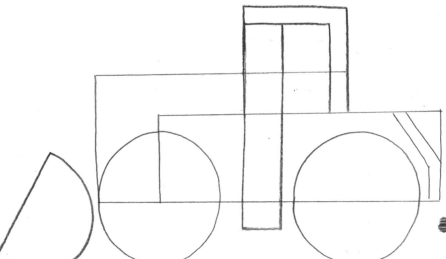

Draw in the shape of the bucket. Add the shape of the driver's cab and steps.

Draw in the complex arm of the digger attached to the bucket. Add two small circles to the centre of the wheels.

Draw in the driver. Add the wheel rims with circles. Add steps and a small exhaust.

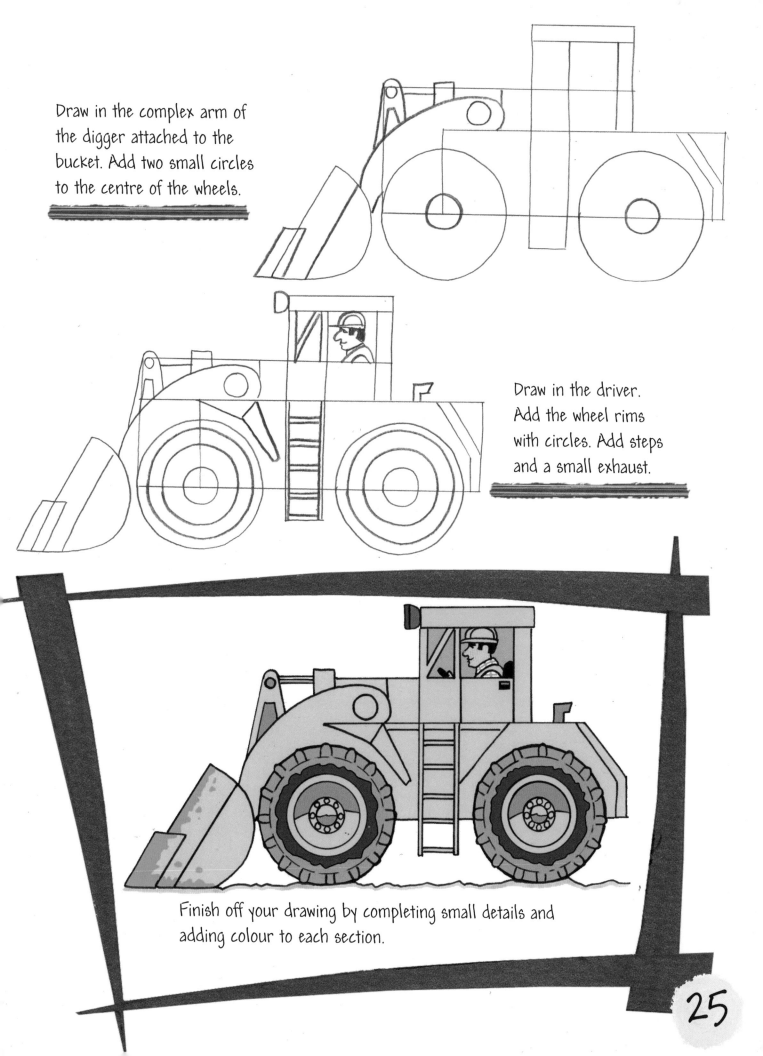

Finish off your drawing by completing small details and adding colour to each section.

25

Fire truck

Fire trucks have to carry a lot of equipment, including an extending ladder, but they still need to be fast enough to reach emergencies quickly.

Draw two circles for wheels. Add a large overlapping rectangle.

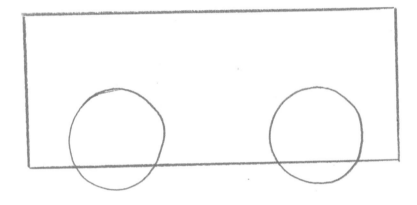

Draw in the front and rear bumpers. Add the shape of the front of the truck and the detail between the wheels.

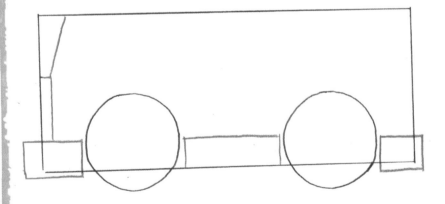

Draw in the wheel arches and two more circles for the hubcaps. Add detail at the rear of the truck.

Using straight lines, draw the ladder on top of the truck and add the detail at the back. Divide the truck body into sections and draw two small circles inside each wheel.

Add a zigzag framework to the ladder. Draw in the windows and add three firemen inside the vehicle. Draw the stripe on the side of the truck and add two different hubcaps.

Complete your drawing by adding all the remaining details and colouring it a bright red!

Earth mover

This giant machine is used for moving vast amounts of earth in open-pit mining operations.

Draw two circles for the wheels and add a rectangle for the chassis of the vehicle.

Copy these shapes to create other sections of the vehicle.

Add more straight lines to extend and complete the main structure.

Draw in the windows and the mudguards and add two more circles inside each of the wheels. Add a circle for the bumper.

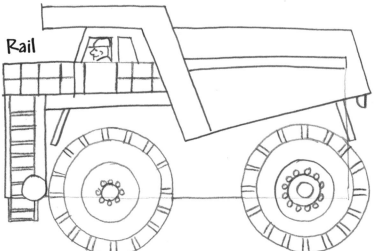

Rail

Draw in the driver and add the rail and ladder. Draw ridges around the edges of each wheel and add wheel nuts.

Your earth mover should be bright yellow. Add a load of earth in the back and brown mud on the wheels.

29

More views

For an extra challenge try drawing your trucks from the front or rear! Practising different views will help you improve your drawing.

Back View

Start with two rectangles for the wheels. Add three horizontal lines.

Draw a rectangle on top and add the cab shape with a curved roof and oval rear window.

Draw in the wooden framework on the back of the truck. Add details underneath.

Add all the little details to finish. A pencil has been used to draw this example. Try other materials to create a different look.

Pickup Truck

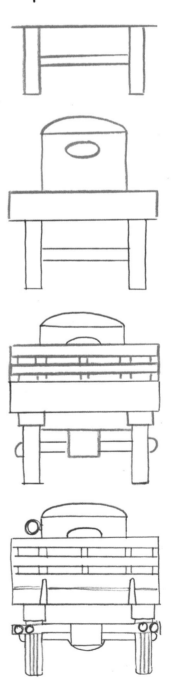

Front View

Start by drawing a rectangle with a line through the centre for the wheel arches and bumper. Add two smaller rectangles for wheels.

Draw in the shape of the cab. Add the window and front grill.

Draw in the windows, the front lights, the grill and the two exhausts.

Finish the front view of the truck by adding these extra details. Then you can colour it in if you want!

Truck

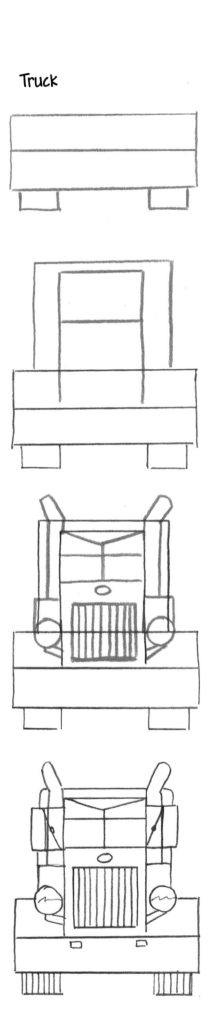

Glossary

bodywork The body of the truck.

cab The part of the truck that the driver sits in.

chassis The frame at the bottom of the main body of a truck.

construction lines Guidelines used in the early stages of a drawing. They are usually erased later.

coupling The part of a truck that links it to its trailer.

exhaust A pipe through which smoke from the engine escapes.

grill A series of slits in the bodywork, near the truck's engine, which allow hot air to escape.

hubcap A metal covering that clips onto the side of a vehicle's wheel.

pneumatic arm A moving mechanism powered by air pressure.

roll bar A safety bar featured in racing vehicles. It protects the driver's head in case of a crash.

shock absorber A device that absorbs the force of sudden, jarring actions.

wheel arches Arches of metal that protect the tops of the wheels.

Index